Never Reorganise Again!

Eddie Obeng

eddie_obeng@pentaclethevbs.com

PentacleTheVBS.com/Never_Reorganise_Again.htm

Copyright © Eddie Obeng 2001

The right of Eddie Obeng to be identified as the author of this work has been asserted in accordance with the Copyright, Designs and Patents Act 1988

First published 2001 by
Pentacle Works The Virtual Media Company
Burke Lodge
20 London End
Beaconsfield
Bucks HP9 2JH

All rights reserved. Except for the quotation of short passages for the purposes of criticism and review, no part of this publication may be reproduced, stored in a retrieval system, or transmitted, in any form or by any means, electronic, mechanical, photocopying, recording or otherwise, without the prior permission of the publisher.

A CIP catalogue record for this book is available from the British Library

ISBN 095348691-5

Typeset by
Sparks Computer Solutions Ltd, Oxford
http://www.sparks.co.uk
Printed and bound by
Alden Press Ltd, Oxford and Northampton

To Susan

My inspiration – always!

Dr Eddie Obeng at Pentacle the Virtual Business School has invented a New Organisation designed for the fast-paced, complex, global New World. An organisation which self organises. Several of Pentacle The Virtual Business School's clients have now implemented this New Organisation over the past six years with impressive results. This book is an introduction and guide to reasons and methods for evolving your current organisation to be in line with the challenges and opportunities you face in your New World.

Eddie Obeng and his team of virtual tutors will work with you and the key executives, managers and leaders in your organisation to help you create the solution for you. Alternatively, you can find out more about the New World management approach and how it applies to your organisation by contacting Pentacle. Dr Obeng also provides regular audio broadcasts/ Webcasts and answers business-specific questions through Pentacle's on-line cyberclubs. If you wish to join other leading thinkers and 'NuvoMondists' who are reinventing their enterprises visit http://pentaclethevbs.com

Pentacle The Virtual Business School
Burke Lodge, 20 London End, Beaconsfield
Bucks HP9 2JH
Tel +44 1494 678 555
Fax +44 1494 671 291
E-mail neveragain@pentaclethevbs.com

Extracts of book on Web
PentacleTheVBS.com/
Never_Reorganise_Again.htm

Web space for discussion
PentacleTheVBS.com/nra.nsf

Cyberclub for organisational developers and human resources professionals
PentacleTheVBS.com/organisationalmagic.htm

Contents

About the Author   xiii

The Petronius Paradox   1

Understanding the Opportunity: New World Organisation   13

Managing the Transition: Breathing Life into your Organisation   93

New Learning in a New Way for a New World: About Pentacle The Virtual Business School   101

E-Clubs: Making Sure that When You're On Your Own You're Not Alone   109

More Copies: Sharing with Others   117

About the Author

EDDIE OBENG pioneered the concept of the NEW WORLD throughout the 1990s. He focuses on helping businesses create and deliver business strategies that allow people to work together to their fullest potential in appropriate virtual organisational structures, using e-enabled information and knowledge to achieve business success in this dynamic New World economy.

Dr Obeng is Founder Director of Pentacle The Virtual Business School (1994), one of the world's most innovative e-learning businesses. He was previously an Executive Director at Ashridge Management College, having begun his career with Shell.

About the Author

Describing his books, *The Daily Telegraph* said, 'He has a backlist of book titles in a style far removed from the ponderous approach of most management tomes'. As the author of a series of books that describe his philosophy for managing in the New World – *New Rules for the New World, All Change!, The Project Leader's Secret Handbook, Putting Strategy to Work, Making Re-engineering Happen, Soundbytes, Achieving Organizational Magic* and *Cybersense* – he writes on the full range of management topics. He is also a major contributor to the *Financial Times Handbook of Management* and *The Gower Handbook of Training and Development*.

In the *Financial Times* he was described as an 'agent provocateur' and a 'leading revolutionary'. *Human Resources* magazine named him as a 'rising guru' and a 'man to watch for the millennium'.

The Daily Telegraph described his as the 'Max Headroom' of the business school world and 'unusual to back his own ideas with his own money'. And *The Sunday Times* described his Pentacle The Virtual Business School as 'one of the few which combine continuous learning with remote management'.

Eddie regularly presents his New World philosophy concepts and success stories to large audiences. His presentations have been described as 'As energetic as Tom Peters but not as long …' (*Human Resources Magazine*).

Eddie is also a regular contributor to journals, magazines and TV.

The Petronius Paradox

Enterprises have always reorganised, adding change to a changing situation and creating chaos … rather than organisation!

Gaius Petronius, writing at a time of rapid change in the Roman Empire, succinctly captured the frustration that reorganisation brings in its wake ...

'WE TRAINED HARD TO MEET OUR CHALLENGES BUT IT SEEMED AS IF EVERY TIME WE WERE BEGINNING TO FORM INTO TEAMS WE WOULD BE RE-ORGANISED. I WAS TO LEARN LATER IN LIFE THAT WE TEND TO MEET ANY NEW SITUATION BY REORGANISING; AND A WONDERFUL METHOD IT CAN BE FOR CREATING THE ILLUSION OF PROGRESS WHILE PRODUCING CONFUSION, INEFFICIENCY AND DEMORALISATION.'

THE PETRONIUS PARADOX

I call the dilemma described above The Petronius Paradox. Times of rapid change can wrong-foot even the best planned organisation. People discover they have to work harder and learn new skills in order to meet the changing demands. This happens long before the enterprise itself realises the need for change. When the enterprise finally wakes up to altering its formal control mechanisms, the most dynamic and 'on-the-ball' individuals in the enterprise will already have learnt how to work around the constraints of an inappropriate system. The formal response may simply spoil its best people's good work. Its reorganisation of resources, reporting lines and responsibilities will disrupt everything that has already been achieved. And worse, because the reorganisation is often called for before the whole problem is understood it may actually not solve the issues it aims to. For many executives the dilemma is not whether to reorganise but when. Failing to reorganise in time may place intolerable strains on your key people – too late and you may destroy the progress they have already made.

The business pressures induced by powerful external shifts mount rapidly. The clamour to 'do something' becomes unbearable. Senior management need a quick win – something tangible, manageable and easy to accomplish. Reorganisation fits the bill exactly. This desire to do something may be bolstered from outside. Advice may be sought from external consultants or pollsters. They analyse the business environment, identify the organisation's strengths and weaknesses, and highlight the need to move resources to seize the opportunities that are available. In short, they propose a reorganisation.

ONE CHANGE LEADS TO ANOTHER.

(Eddie's first law of change.)

As we experience the effects of change we are tempted to add more, unhelpful change. I have noticed that this problem affects widely differing enterprises in the New World economy in a relatively consistent manner. This means that although businesses believe that they face individual and unique problems there is a strong similarity between both the problems and many of the solutions they need to adopt. Strangely, as they try to cope with change they ignore my second law of change,[1] **'Adding Change to Change creates Chaos'**, and simply add to the turbulence that they are experiencing, closing an inevitable vicious cycle.

ADDING CHANGE TO CHANGE
CREATES CHAOS.

(Eddie's second law of change.)

BEYOND THE PETRONIUS PARADOX

Unfortunately, at the pace of change of the New World, **the 'shelf life'(and implementation time) of any particular set of reporting lines is longer than the lifetime of the issue it addresses**. All you can achieve with a conventional reorganisation is to chase your own tail, adding your own Petronius effect to the change around you. Strangely, many executives persist with this approach even though they know that, on average, reorganisation can close to double staff turnover rates and that there is no universal published correlation between reorganisation and subsequent business performance.

This book is about moving beyond this paradox. It's about moving in line and in step with the demands and requirements of the New World. Breaking free of the Petronius Paradox means you must answer when, how often and how to organise for a rapidly changing e-enabled world.

The New World solution to the paradox is to organise – Now, Once, and Virtually.

And now the 21st-century version:

'WE LEARNT FAST TO BENEFIT FROM THE OPPORTUNITIES AROUND US AND IT SEEMED AS IF EVERY TIME WE WERE STARTING TO FORM FIXED HABITS AROUND OBSOLETE KNOWLEDGE AND WORKING PRACTICES WE WOULD REALIGN OURSELVES, OUR TEAMS AND OUR NETWORKS. I WAS TO LEARN LATER IN LIFE THAT BY BUILDING ENJOYABLE AND TRUSTING RELATIONSHIPS ALIGNING WITH SHARED DREAMS AND MAKING SURE THAT INFORMATION NEEDED IS PROVIDED, AND BY WORKING WITH A WIDE RANGE OF PEOPLE, I COULD ACHIEVE FULFILMENT IN MY ROLE AND ENSURE THAT THE ENTERPRISE WAS ROBUST AND EFFECTIVE.

I hope you will enjoy this book and that it will not only challenge your thinking but also provide you with real answers.

I would like to thank key leaders in the following organisations, without whom this book would not have been written: Novartis, Sony, Nortel, GlaxoWellcome, Microsoft, Mercury (Cable & Wireless), Enodis (Magnet), Boots Properties, Motorola, SmithKlineBeecham and Amersham International.

Eddie Obeng
Burke Lodge
April 2001

NOTE

1. Obeng (1994) *All Change*, Financial Times Publishing, ISBN 0273 62221 8.

Understanding the Opportunity:

New World Organisation

The New World[1] of business[2] is now fully upon us all. Leaders of organisations are coming to recognise that the New World extends well beyond the publicised and high-profile e-activities and 'dotcoms' to all their internal and external activities. They are beginning to realise that the speed of change, levels of complexity and the speed of information have irrevocably altered the businessphere[3] of operation.

So, *the challenge* – speed, agility,[4] developing new capabilities, retaining talent, global virtual teaming, intelligent products, mass customisation[5] of customer relationships, reach.

The solution – new business models, use of cyberspace,[6] especially the Internet, local involvement of global leaders, new offerings delivered in new ways to new customers,[7] $24 \times 7 \times 365 \times$ Worldwide – business empires on which the sun never sets, clicks and mortar – marriage of touchspace[8] and cyberspace. Altogether exciting, new and untried.

The paradox – how to stay in control in a business environment which demands that you create new ways of operating which no one yet fully understands.[9] The simplest way to understand the paradox is through an 'odd-one-out' quiz.

New World Organisation

Which of these is the odd-one-out?

1. Run a formula one car using a steam engine.

2. Power a Boeing 737 with a water wheel.

3. Run a notebook computer using transistors.

4. Fuel a laser-guided smart bomb with gunpowder.

5. Drive the screen of a palm pilot using valves.

6. Organise a new world global business model using a 100-year-old command-and-control hierarchical structure.

Did you guess right? Most people guess that number six is the odd one out. But why is it the odd one out?

The reason – not because it's funny, not because it's obviously the only one related to the topic being discussed here, not because it's the only one that spills onto four lines of text, but because it is the only one out of the six that we actually try to do!

Because we are aware that there is an anomaly, a significant amount of academic thought has gone into rethinking how enterprises and businesses should organise their people.[10–14] However, in reality, there is little evidence of enterprises actually changing their traditional approach.

But it is not just because our thinking on how to organise is old that we need to reinvent it. There are a number of other reasons.

THE NEW WORLD

Over the past decade, for many enterprises, the pace of change in their businessphere easily outstrips the speed at which the organisation can learn or respond to the change. As this happens, business forecasts become more difficult to achieve or sustain, market capitalisation valuations become less easily understood, the enterprise finds itself constantly under pressure to reorganise or merge – either to align resources to take advantage of recently identified opportunities, or to avoid unanticipated threats and issues. The enterprise finds itself investing substantially in technologies or activities in which it has little historical experience.

This is the evidence of the transition from the Old World to the New. Miles Flint, President of Sony Broadcast and Professional Europe reflected that, 'In Sony our old world of analogue technology sold through a country-based channel needed to be replaced by a European digital solution-based approach.'[15]

The drivers of this transition are already well documented and understood – technology, aspirations/expectations, new economics – especially information economics, global reach.[16] What is less well documented is the impact on old assumptions about the best way to run a successful enterprise.

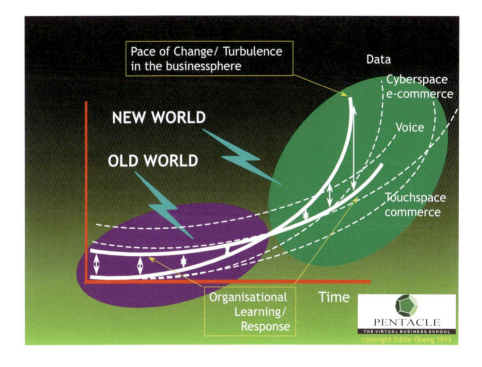

1 Business model

In their simplest form Old World enterprises are usually based around a simple business model. They rely on few entities (customers, suppliers, etc.), there is a simple flow of money usually in exchange for goods (or services (or information)). The focus is on the ability to provide superior offerings at the expense of directly competing offers. The offers are based around a small range of technologies and are labelled as an industry. Diversified or divisional enterprises added a layer of financial control on top of this model to allow the management of the additional complexity through simpler financial measurements.

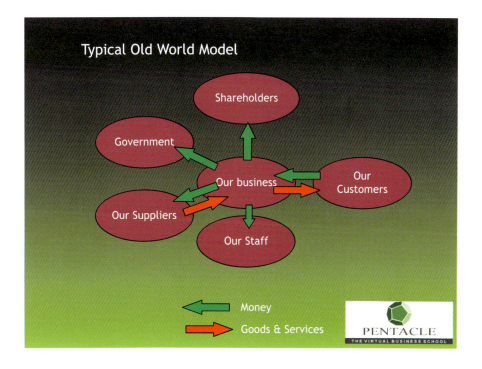

Success is based around doing 'more-of-the-same', building on experience and exporting the offer to as many people as reachable. Because of scale advantages and reduced risk of repeated activity in a relatively stable market/industry the 'winning' company generally gains the largest share of market and highest customer loyalty, best supplier infrastructure and can generate superior profits as a result of this. In addition the dominance created by the lead player/players plus the difficulty for customers to easily identify alternative offers leads to additional financial performance. (Without the Internet it is impossible to do a global search on suppliers of a particular product so you buy on name rather than value.)

New World enterprises tend to be based around complex or unusual models often involving knowledge rights or retention. There are complex flows of money. Often goods (or services (or information)) are provided to one entity and paid for by a separate entity. The focus is on providing a faster and more comprehensive or value-adding offering.

Often direct competitors are identified as enterprises satisfying the same **need** – not just producing the same product/offer. However, because of the increasingly multitudinous ways of satisfying each specific need it becomes more relevant to consider enterprises influencing or influenced by the same entities as being in the same 'businessphere' rather than industry.

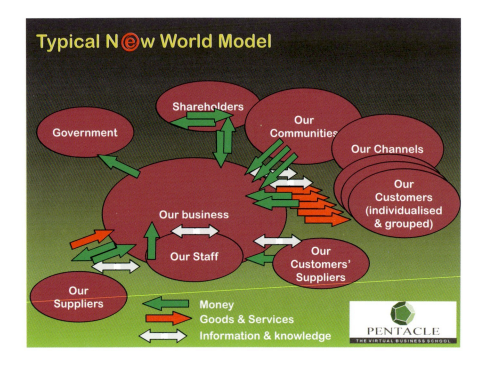

Success is based on a combination of providing new offerings in a different way, old offerings in a different way and new offerings in a traditional way. In general, success 'raises the bar' and leads to a need to extend the business model in order to further improve performance. Innovative use of touchspace and cyberspace alter the cost of operations and the scale achievable. Active use of information economics – replication, network effects, bootstrapping – often leads to explosive exponential growth.

New and more complex business models, with multiple channels to the customer, consumer or client supported by complex strategic alliances need a clear organisational map that helps people work together flexibly.

2 Capturing and sharing knowledge

In the Old World a year really was a short time. It was the basis of the budgeting cycle – a reasonable planning and implementation horizon. Why was it a short time? Because in an environment focused on doing more-of-the-same, the few different or unanticipated issues that did occur were widely spread and did not cross-influence each other. As a result, knowledge acquired had a significant 'shelf life'. The net result was that in an enterprise, the people with the longest experience of the industry were best placed to make strategic and tactical decisions. Knowledge was held at the 'top' of the organisation which was also where all the key controls on resourcing and finance were held. By ensuring that the bulk of the people in the enterprise did what was demanded of them by the ones with the most knowledge, the security of an enterprise was and is best assured. As a result the management at the top closely determined the actions and focus of the rest of the organisation. In order to deal with complexity, decisions and issues were aligned by function or segmented by department or division. As the bulk of activity was repetitive and based on prior knowledge, little information was required to flow up or down the organisation. In addition, the volume of information flowing into the organisation was low, often limited to structured market research, etc.

Most enterprises adopted the concept of 'reporting', an expression borrowed from quite an ancient Naval heritage – imagine the scenario circa 1700, on a wooden ship in a rough sea. The captain (the one with the knowledge and experience) wants a change to a sail at the other end of the ship – far away from the bridge where he is standing.

What does he do? Well, he could shout an instruction but it is likely that the wind would carry his command away and it wouldn't be heard. Instead he orders the officer standing a few feet from him. The officer passes the message on – down a long 'chain of command' until the order reaches the crewman responsible for the rope. The action is carried out, and then the crewman 'reports' back up the chain so that the captain knows it has been done and can now make the next decision. Great system, but what has it got to do with a modern business enterprise? We are no longer forced to pass messages by word of mouth down a long chain. For that we have cyberspace – phones, faxes, emails and so on – which allow us to communicate directly wherever we are in the world.

THE BEST PERSON TO DO IT
SHOULD DO IT –
WITHOUT DUPLICATION.

An important but little recognised fact is that information velocity, the maximum speed with which we can move units of data, increases faster than the rate of computing power. Many managers will be familiar with Moore's law, which suggests a doubling of computing power every 18 months. Information goes faster – up by a factor of 10 every 3 years. Why is this important? It is important because there is a maximum speed at which a group of people can absorb information. Assuming a top management team of 25, in conversations the limit is about 1 Mb/s.[17] This rate is fixed – true, you can get more out of your 1 Mb/s by concentrating on information – on answers rather than data – by making information graphical and colour based, by using audible warnings, etc., but there is still a limit. Why is this a problem? Well, it wasn't. In the Old World this velocity was more than adequate. In the New World, though, the problem starts at a local level where the simple speed around a local area network is two to three orders of magnitude faster than this maximum speed to reach the 'top management' – it is much faster to go across or around the organisation than up it. The problem is amplified because the global/wide area networks also operate at one to two orders of magnitude of the speed to management. Fast but slower than the local traffic. Nonetheless, a significant amount of information flows to and from the organisation via the Internet, telephone conversations and so on.

Traditional/formal 'reporting structure'

Reality of direct connections to people who need the information

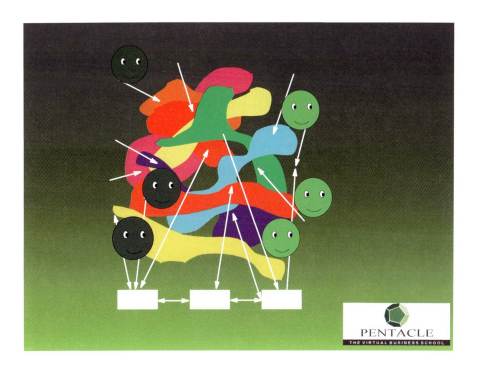

Many people find that they are members of multiple teams and processes.

IN MOST ORGANISATIONS EFFECTIVE MANAGERS HAVE THEIR OWN 'PRIVATE DIRECT ACCESS NETWORK' – TO ALLOW THEM TO COLLECT AND SEND INFORMATION AS DIRECTLY AS POSSIBLE TO THE PEOPLE WHO NEED IT. THEY OPERATE A VERSION OF EMPOWERMENT WHICH IS TWO CROSSED FINGERS HOPING THAT THE ORGANISATION WILL NOT FORMALLY REVERSE THE SUCCESSES THEY HAVE MADE.

All this leads to two frightening conclusions. First, the flow of information to the top management of a globally distributed organisation will/has become a bottleneck to decisions and focus. Second, the flow of synergistic/knowledge management from one local operation or function through a formal process via top management to other local operations or functions will not work.

In most organisations effective managers have their own 'private direct access network' – to allow them to collect and send information as directly as possible to the people who need it. They operate a version of empowerment that is two crossed fingers hoping that the organisation will not formally reverse the successes they have made.

3 *Movement and realignment of resource*

The third reason for the need to change is the increasingly debilitating effect of what I describe as the Petronius[18] Paradox. At the pace of change suffered by organisations in the New World, it is difficult to sustain alignment of functional or divisional resources on the key priorities for very long. This leads to a constant reorganisation cycle that is often exacerbated if there is rapid turnover of key executives. Furthermore, organisations who are unable to cope with the pace of the New World have two legitimate options: 'accelerate' or 'die'. But they often choose a third option – 'get really big and dominate the market place, then we won't need to go faster'. This strategy drives the logic of consolidation affecting most businesspheres. Mergers and acquisitions have in the New World become part of 'business as usual'.

THE 'SHELF LIFE' (AND IMPLEMENTATION TIME) OF ANY PARTICULAR SET OF REPORTING LINES IS LONGER THAN THE LIFETIME OF THE ISSUE IT ADDRESSES.

Every acquisition or merger, unless innovatively handled, simply leads on to additional pressure for realigning resources. In theory the process should be quick – instantaneous even! In practice, because of the impact of reorganisation on the status of individuals, their potential power, positions and therefore relationships, their potential career opportunities, their role in the organisation – and especially if they still have one after reorganisation – far from being a quick logical process it is a slow, emotional roller-coaster that takes months, if not years, to fade into the background noise of personal and organisational priorities.

Realignment of resources and people's roles and priorities in the New World should not be so intricately linked with power, position and personal opportunity, but instead it should be directly related to the current/future challenge or business opportunity and should allow individuals in the company to use their attitudes and capabilities to fulfil their potential.

4 Management/leadership balance

The final driver is the change in emphasis of the behaviours within the enterprise. Old World enterprises, with their focus on experience and procedure, could be effectively driven through standard management practices based on past activities. New or innovative challenges had, as always, to be led. The role of leadership was given to the senior managers – which it had to be, since with their powerful control levers they could actively prevent any change led from elsewhere in the enterprise. **Leadership and management came from the top**.

In the New World the enterprise's agenda includes significant change, demanding a higher level of leadership. However, as most senior management teams are now bottlenecks suffering data or information overload, often relying on past and now obsolete experience, they may not be the best people to lead the change in many circumstances. So **leadership shifts from the 'top' to 'whoever is in front'** – and that might be anybody, right down to the new recruit with knowledge on particular protocols!

NOT A MATRIX - A NEW DIMENSION

The death knell of the old 'Command-and-Control' hierarchy has sounded often before. As early as the last century, in the 1970s, enterprises were experimenting with 'matrix organisations'. Success was limited because the duplication of the command-and-control structure that ensued allowed the creation of an intensely political and bureaucratic operating and working environment, and a mish-mash of confusing and confused accountabilities and responsibilities. Furthermore, the information requirements to sustain a matrix organisation are tremendous and in the last century there were few tools capable of providing the information transparency required. The experiments usually ended as disappointments.[19]

With the cyberspace and touchspace opportunities the New World gives us, it is possible to give ourselves another approach. However, any attempt to suggest a working organisational framework must satisfy certain conditions if it is to be practical and to be viewed with any sense of reality.

Conditions for a New Organisation for a New World

- Enterprise objectives match – the organisational framework must recognise that enterprises exist usually to generate money for some of the key entities[20] of the business model.

- Allow personal aspiration, commitment, growth and development – without compromise.

- Ease of explanation – like the Old World 'garden fork' used to explain a hierarchy, the framework should be visually simple and easy to communicate to all from the new undergraduate recruit to the global chairman.[21]

- Scalability – the framework should be capable of being interpreted at all levels of scale: individual, local team, global team, local enterprise, global enterprise, multi-global enterprise.

- Resilience, flexibility and adaptability – must not be compromised.

- Comprehensiveness – the framework should be capable of fitting the majority of New World enterprises without additional modification.

... Your last re-organisation ever ...

In order to break the Petronius Paradox it is essential to build an organising framework that is designed, not around command and control, but instead **around the key elements of an enterprise that remain constant in a changing business environment**. The model must be complex enough to deal with the real issues involved but not complicated. It must be simple enough to be easily communicated and usable by all the people in the enterprise. It must recognise the interconnectedness of the various entities in the enterprise and allow for the effective flow of information within it.

NEW AND MORE COMPLEX BUSINESS MODELS, WITH MULTIPLE CHANNELS TO THE CUSTOMER, CONSUMER OR CLIENT SUPPORTED BY COMPLEX STRATEGIC ALLIANCES, NEED A CLEAR ORGANISATIONAL MAP WHICH HELPS PEOPLE WORK TOGETHER FLEXIBLY.

The framework described below, which I've named immodestly the Obeng OrganoWeb or Obeng's O-Web (although my clients have referred to it as the Organisational Grid[22] or the Pointed Star or the Organisational Pentagon), has now been successfully implemented in several *Fortune* 500 organisations described elsewhere.[23] At Pentacle we often refer to the transition from the traditional hierachichal reporting approach to the network/team/individual connected OrganoWeb as 'the last reorganisation ever'. Geoff Hall, Vice President of Technology at Nortel, said when they implemented the OrganoWeb that,[23] 'We aimed to make the natural way of working the actual way of working.' This reference explains how the formal structure of Obeng's OrganoWeb closely mimics the work-arounds and more effective informal links and connections through which the bulk of organisational work is actually done.

New World Organisation 49

It is difficult to understand Obeng's OrganoWeb without looking at the issue of helping people clarify where and how they contribute to the whole in a slightly different way. The traditional organisational hierarchy relies on chains of command and control – lines of accountability/responsibility where the person who is responsible for the individual as a resource is also the person to whom they are accountable. (It is assumed that they are the recipient of your output, that is, it is assumed that you work for your boss.)

In order to understand the framework imagine that the classic organogram is being laid flat on a surface.

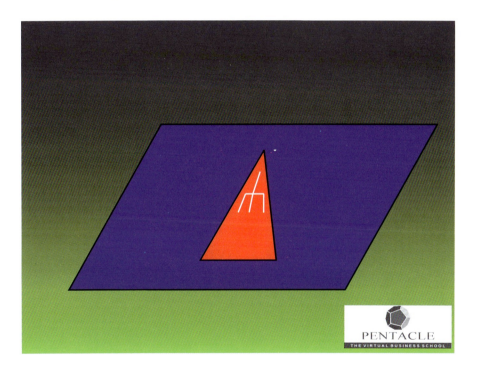

This small adjustment allows us to think in more than just two dimensions. Firstly we can split out **accountability** – who the output is intended for – away from **responsibility** – who has the authority to allow a response. Following this, day-to-day activities are considered as taking place above the page.

SEPARATE ACCOUNTABILITY AND RESPONSIBILITY. FOCUS ACCOUNTABILITY ON THE PURPOSE.

The OrganoWeb is best understood by thinking in a third dimension.

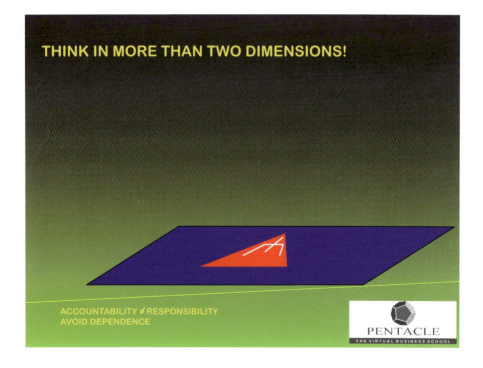

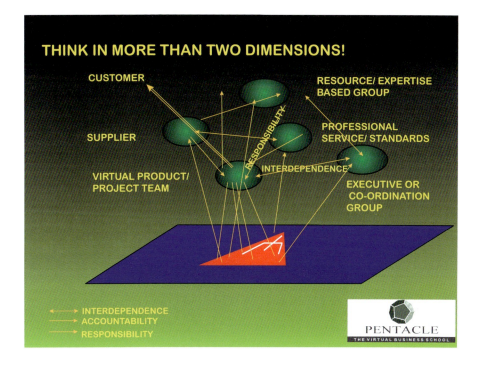

To simplify the description, concentrate on the groupings of people required to achieve the outcomes and their roles.

In the arrangement on the previous pages, people and resources are aligned to deliver to customer needs (follow the direction of the accountability arrows). Responsibility for resources is also aligned. The whole virtual organisation is coordinated through interdependence.

If you follow the arrows you will discover that activities are aligned to deliver a result to the customer entity. Some of the lines have double arrowheads. This will be explained later and simply represents co-ordination.

PEOPLE CREATE CHANGE –
PEOPLE CONSTRAIN CHANGE.

We base our model on what we refer to as 'dimensions' of an organisation. These dimensions include all the anticipated activities and sociological requirements of the organisation

For a business enterprise with a goal of making money, the dimensions can be grouped around six purposes:

- making money through processes and projects;

- offering solution development and relationship management;

- providing strategic and personal leadership, co-ordination, delivering change and an appropriate working culture;

- high-quality internal application of professional services;

- gaining access to appropriate suppliers/alliances and partnerships, and a virtual network;

- delivering current core capabilities, developing excellence in future capabilities and providing opportunities for people to contribute fully and grow.

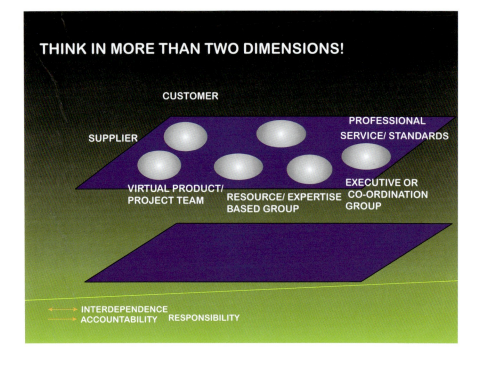

In order to re-simplify the OrganoWeb for communication we re-establish a two dimensional view. Only one of each of the key groupings is shown. In practice, the number and size of each virtual team is dependent on the organisational needs and challenges. In addition it is important to recognise that new requirements or redundant activities are easily dealt with simply by adding or removing virtual teams as required.

Christophe Gillet, of Sony's Business Innovation Business Team, described this, 'We start with a blank sheet of paper and have the complete freedom of initiative. Having a bunch of people who are creating their own mission is very new in Sony'.[23]

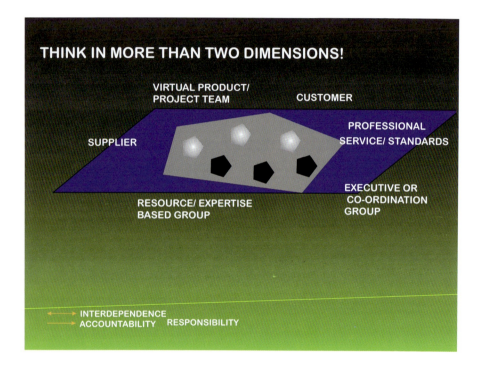

The people groups are bounded by external interfaces represented by the pentagon. In many organisations this boundary represents the people who are completely contracted into the organisation emotionally and legally.

Back in two dimensions showing the virtual and core teams as white pentagons.

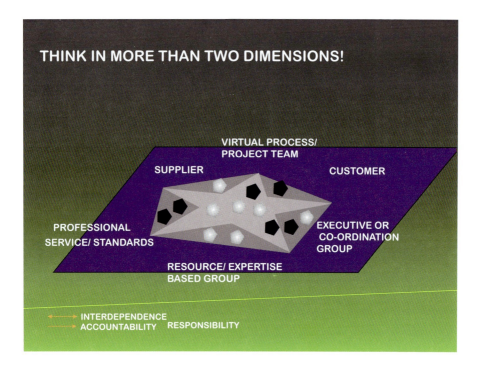

Each real life implementation Pentacle has carried out has resulted in a different mix and number of virtual and core teams.

In order to make interpretation easier the six areas are separated – with the money making processes and projects central to the model. Unlike the traditional organisation which represents as its purpose, control and command, the OrganoWeb's pentagon centres on the purpose of the enterprise as a whole – making money.

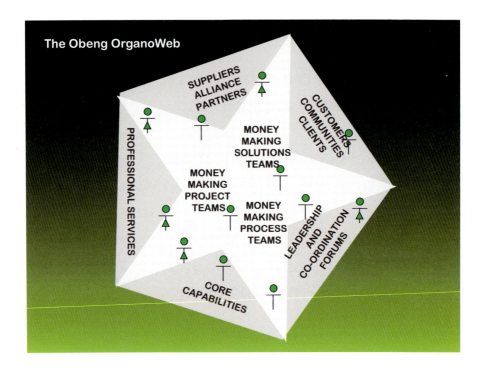

In real implementations it is common for some people's names to appear in more than one place. These people, nicknamed 'nodes', are essential for the effective functioning of the organisation.

The complete OrganoWeb shows you where people are, their primary role and also shows the virtual teams and the areas they are accountable or responsible for.

The OrganoWeb can be applied at an individual, team, enterprise, regional or global level without requiring additional explanation. Many people in the O-Web will find their names in more than one area.

The old functional organisation was based around the Sloan-based manufacturing process, and as a result the functions – sales, marketing, manufacturing, etc. – never quite mapped onto the actual requirements of customers, strategic partners, stakeholders and employees.

The next diagram shows how the O-Web easily maps onto a new world business model of multiple entities and relationships.

And since it is relatively straightforward to add virtual or core teams depending on the actual need, any market space can be effectively mapped to.

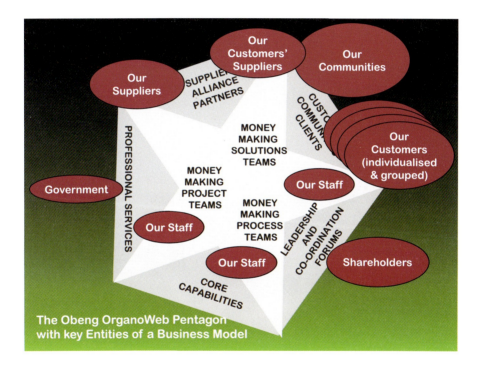

The Obeng OrganoWeb Pentagon with key Entities of a Business Model

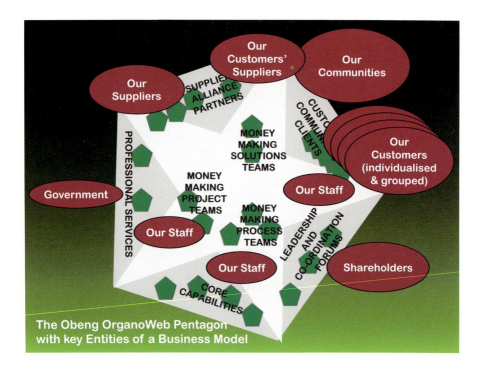

The Obeng OrganoWeb Pentagon with key Entities of a Business Model

It is important to map virtual/core teams to the actual needs of the business model.

Individuals, virtual teams or networks accountable for the various entities are agreed through a process of reviewing and investigating how the entity is best managed.

The internal O-Web focuses on the people within the organisation and how they relate to each other. A good design can effectively account for other entities via the accountabilities of the virtual teams.

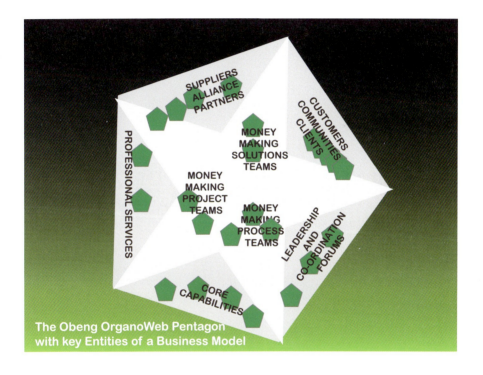
The Obeng OrganoWeb Pentagon with key Entities of a Business Model

THE EFFECT IS MORE IMPORTANT
THAN THE FORM.

MAKING THE OBENG ORGANOWEB WORK IN PRACTICE

Simply drawing a strange shape covered in small green pentagons is not going to recreate the working habits of all the people in the organisation. In addition, there are a number of practical activities and new assumptions, which the people engaged in making it work are going to have to understand and work to.

O-WEB PREREQUISITES

There are five prerequisites to the realistic and effective functioning of the Obeng OrganoWeb.

1. Interdependence

2. Separate accountability and responsibility. Focus accountability on the purpose.

3. Federalism: the best person to do it should do it without duplication

4. Virtuality: the effect is more important than the form

5. Control must never outweigh leadership

1 Interdependence

Because of the potential for complexity in the model it is important to cross-link as many entities into systems as possible. Since there are always fewer systems than entities this not only simplifies running the organisation but also reduces the need to police activities. In addition it makes it more difficult for non-moneymaking political activities to be added unwittingly to the agenda.

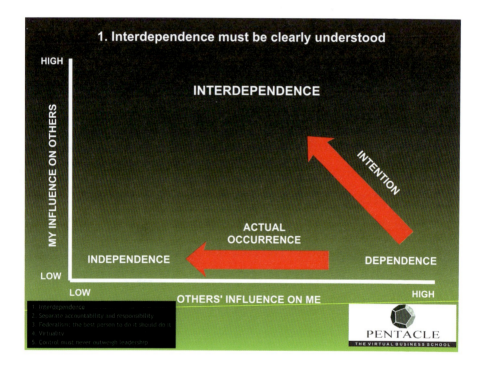

2 *Separate accountability and responsibility. Focus accountability on the purpose*

By ensuring that the accountabilities of every key role are clearly understood and set up, there is less opportunity for internal conflict. In addition, provided that the accountabilities are focused on money making activities, the 'flow of money'/resource allocated to delivery of the offerings or solutions is simply in the opposite direction to the flow of accountabilities.

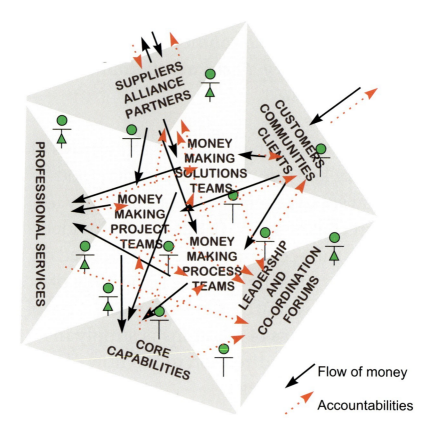

3 Federalism: the best person to do it should do it - without duplication

This rule is best supported by the creation of transparent internal activities – the use of an intranet to ensure that there is not unwitting addition of complexity or duplication. Jacques Racloz, then Chief Executive of Novartis Pharmaceuticals, said, 'Federalism is essential to success. It allows alignment without confusion and internal fighting.'[24]

4 Virtuality: the effect is more important than the form

The active use of virtual structures, particularly virtual teams as a way of providing the agility and flexibility required, become common. The diagram to the right helps explain the difference between virtual team working and traditional units.

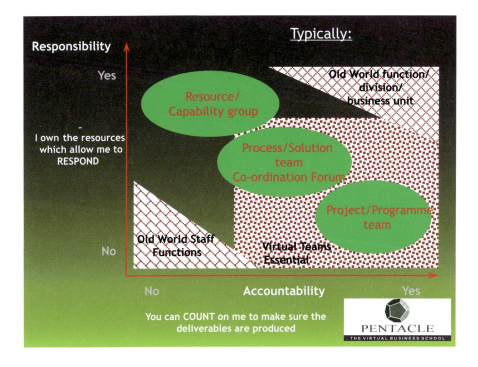

MOVE FROM DEPENDENCE TO INTERDEPENDENCE (NOT INDEPENDENCE).

5 *Control must never outweigh leadership*

Control is the hallmark of the Old World whilst leadership is a measure of the New. If control is the first instinct most of the decisions made will not be based on a full understanding to the actual situation. Furthermore rather than empowering the people in the organisation and ensuring that you gain their engagement and commitment you will systematically be reintroducing the disempowerment of the old hierarchy.

CONTROL MUST NEVER OUTWEIGH LEADERSHIP.

CONCLUSIONS

Over the past six years a number of organisations have put into place and benefited from the implementation of the Obeng OrganoWeb pentagon. Each implementation has been different and unique – completely dependent on the organisation's situation and strategic imperatives. Each of these implementations has been heavily dependent on the visionary leadership of key individuals.[25] This book is dedicated to the courage and determination of these New World Pioneers.

NOTES

1. Obeng & Crainer (1995) *Making Re-engineering happen*, Financial Times Management Publishing, London, ISBN 0 273 62220, p. 39.

2. Crainer (1999) *The Financial Times Handbook of Management*, Financial Times Publishing, London, ISBN 0273 60694 8, p. 173.

3. A businessphere is a group of enterprises influenced by or influencing the same entities, e.g. customer types, technology providers, regulatory groups, etc.

4. Hamel & Prahalad (1994) Competing for the Future, Harvard Business School Press, ISBN 0 87584 416 2.

5. Peters (1997) *Circle of Innovation*, Hodder & Stoughton, London, ISBN 0 340 71720 3.

6. Negroponte (1996) *Being Digital*, Hodder & Stoughton, ISBN 0 340 64930 5.

7. Pappows (1998) *Enterprise.com*, Nicholas Brealey, London, ISBN 1 85788 207 5.

8. Obeng (1997) *New Rules for the New World*, Capstone, Oxford, ISBN 1 900961 15 6, p. 10.

9   Obeng (1997) *New Rules for the New World*, Capstone, Oxford, ISBN 1 900961 15 6.

10 Hammer & Stanton (1999) 'How process enterprises really work', *Harvard Business Review*, November–December.

11 Mintzberg & Van der Heyden (1999) 'Organigraphs', *Harvard Business Review*, September–October.

12 Grenier & Metes (1995) *Going Virtual*, Prentice Hall, New Jersey, ISBN 0 13 185299 X.

13 Ross & Kay (1994) *Toppling the Pyramids*, Time Books, ISBN 0 8129 2341 3.

14 Hedberg, Dahlgren, Hansson & Olve (1997) *Virtual Organisations and Beyond*, John Wiley, London, ISBN 0 471 97493 5.

15 Obeng & Flint (1998) Leadership presentation, Frontiers of Change Conference, Impact.

16 Obeng (1997) *New Rules for the New World*, Capstone, Oxford, ISBN 1 900961 15 6.

17 Source: Kevin Baughan, Nortel Networks, 2000.

18 Petronius was a Roman Centurion to whom the quote that follows is usually attributed. 'We trained hard. We trained hard to meet our challenges but it seemed as if every time we

were beginning to form into teams we would be reorganised. I was to learn later in life that we tend to meet any new situation by reorganising; and a wonderful method it can be for creating the illusion of progress while producing confusion, inefficiency and demoralisation.'

19 'All the power but none of the Glory' – William Hall On Goran Lindahl at ABB scrapping Percy Barnevik's much acclaimed Matrix structure and returning to a hierarchy, *Financial Times*, 24 August 1999.

20 Obeng (2000) Mapping Business Models, Pentacle Works.

21 In a recent experiment I circulated an HBR article (Mintzberg (1999) 'Organigraphs', Harvard Business Review, September) on organisation to executives of a global food equipment company to demonstrate the current academic thinking. The response to the 18-page article was one of disbelief on the complexity of the models and the impossibility of communicating such complex models to the whole organisation.

22 The model implemented by Novartis Pharmaceuticals did not include the supplier dimension and was named 'the grid' by the Executive team.

23 Margaret Coles, *Sunday Times*, 28 May 2000.

24 Source: Kick-off conference for the new Organisational Grid, Brighton, 1997.

25 Jacques Racloz, Jeanette Swan, Miles Flint, Pete Floyd, Geoff Hall, Neil Stewart, Tony Wareing, Howard Pien, David Williams, Jill Hughes, Ian Farman, Peter Felton, Peter Harlow, Diane Jones, Gerard Blanc, Steve Whyard, Chris Henderson, Peter Baguley.

REALIGNMENT OF RESOURCES AND PEOPLE'S ROLES AND PRIORITIES IN THE NEW WORLD SHOULD NOT BE SO INTRICATELY LINKED WITH POWER, POSITION AND PERSONAL OPPORTUNITY, BUT INSTEAD IT SHOULD BE DIRECTLY RELATED TO THE CURRENT/FUTURE CHALLENGE OR BUSINESS OPPORTUNITY AND SHOULD ALLOW INDIVIDUALS IN THE COMPANY TO USE THEIR ATTITUDES AND CAPABILITIES TO FULFIL THEIR POTENTIAL.

Managing the transition:

Breathing Life into your Organisation

Although a clear transition plan is described below, in practice the process tends to be closer to 'walking through the fog' than 'painting by numbers'. The reason is that it is difficult for people to initially grasp the wholesale change in thinking and behaving and systems that the transition demands. As a result although there is general agreement on what we are changing from few people can accurately describe how what we are changing *to* will look, how it will feel or how it will operate at a practical level.

NOT A MATRIX – A NEW DIMENSION.

A second headache is that although the steps are described – e.g. understanding business model – in most situations many of the people involved are often even unsure about what a business model actually is. It is common to go over the same ground a number of times as individuals in the implementation team learn about what is required. So not only are we unclear on the goal but also on the method. The overall fogginess generally leads to an emotional rollercoaster of a ride in managing the transition.

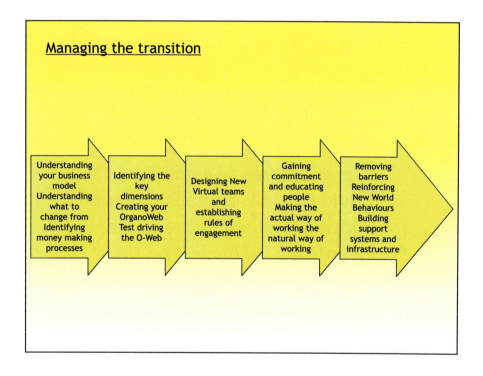

It is recommended that implementation be managed using the New World project management approach for foggy projects.[1]

The key characteristics of the approach to successfully managing a foggy project are the steady drumbeat of frequent meetings/reviews/planning sessions involving as wide a range of stakeholders as possible.

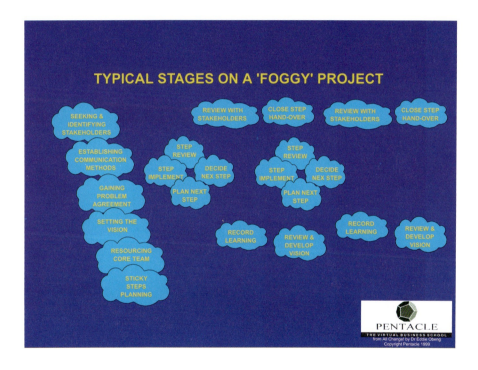

Take care in selecting the transition project leader and core team and sponsor. Not only do you need an appropriate cross section of opinion leaders from across the organisation but also you need people who are comfortable with leading others through the Fog.

Note

1 Obeng (1995) *Putting Strategy to Work*, Financial Times Publishing, London, 0 273 60265 9.

New Learning in a New Way for a New World:

About Pentacle
The Virtual Business School

SUPPORTING ORGANISATIONS IMPLEMENTING STRATEGIC CHANGE

Pentacle The Virtual Business School is unlike any other. It provides a continuous link between learning and the implementation of leading ideas and management approaches. Such an ongoing relationship is best served through our 'network' of experts and by constant communication with clients. Pentacle The Virtual Business School itself operates as a virtual structure, moulding itself around client needs. Course members, executives and managers use short, modular learning events, our secure intranet, the Internet and our business simulations to update and test their knowledge and skills. Direct access to our coaches allows them to apply what they are learning directly to their jobs wherever they are in the world. Subject areas essential for effectiveness in the New World include:

- leadership thinking and behaviour;
- strategy and future orientation;
- change and project management;
- information and knowledge management and deployment;
- virtual or self-directed team working;
- programme management;
- market and customer focus; and
- developing critical processes.

'Learning and doing worked hand in hand to break new ground. It gave us an enormous feeling of satisfaction that we had broken new ground for Motorola and proved how effective virtual teams can be in producing leading edge results.'

Motorola

'Converted to the New World!'

Pharmaceutical client

PRACTISING WHAT WE PREACH

A recent bench marking exercise on The Virtual Business School versus traditional Business Schools concluded with the statistics below:

Ratio: variable to fixed costs

Traditional – 1:8   Virtual – 3:1

Ratio: theoretical knowledge input to skills and application

Traditional – 4:1   Virtual – 1:2

Ratio: educators and experts to support

Traditional – 1:5   Virtual – 1:2

DEVELOPING NEW WAYS TO LEARN

In addition, Eddie has pioneered the development of new types of business simulations to allow organisations to understand and test the effect of the New World on their thinking and behaviour. Pentacle The Virtual Business School created the first business simulation in three-dimensional virtual reality. *Columbus* is a way of examining and redesigning internal processes profitably.

> *'Examining business processes requires a tool which shows how they flow through the business. Seeing how all the various processes interact on screen (or in the screen) brings it all to life and makes it easier to take the broader perspective.'*
>
> Senior line manager
> Utilities company

HELPING YOU CREATE YOUR WORLD-BEATING VIRTUAL ORGANISATION STRUCTURE

Pentacle also offers the service of helping other organisations set up virtual organisations and even other virtual learning organisations such as in-company virtual universities. We are helping major business organisations create pan-European organisational structures, re-designing sales and marketing organisations to make them customer facing rather than product focused and integrating manufacturing structures across Europe.

About Pentacle The Virtual Business School

What do these logos have in Common?

Living Virtual Organisations for Global or Pan European or National businesses based on Eddie Obeng's revolutionary New World Management Approach

E-Clubs:

Making Sure that When You're On Your Own You're Not Alone

Why join a club?

> To help you transform ideas into reality – To learn – To share issues – To steal ideas – To gain access to useful tools for the job – To have a live coach – To find out how good you are compared to the rest of the world – To have someone help diagnose your issues – To get some space to think – To be trendy and cool – To bounce ideas – To find out what the latest New World thinking is …

What do I get?

The club rooms in each club area follow a similar structure. You will get: a **library** of materials, frequently asked questions and learning bytes; a **notice board** for the latest news; a **surgery** (where you go for personal coaching); a **tool room** (containing practical tools and techniques you can use in your real job); a **games room** containing self learning simulations for you to test your knowledge and skills on; a **work room** containing free or hosted access to Pentacle software to support you in your role and job; a **radio room** where you can listen to the weekly 'latest news' broadcast by **Franck** and to specific answers to posted questions; a **shop** selling hardware and software which you can use along with reviews on the latest products; a **coffee lounge/bar** area where you can network; and **meeting rooms** for smaller groups who want to work on a particular topic or issue. If you can think of anything we've missed let us know.

What clubs are available?

There are 12 clubs covering most of the issues people routinely face in the New World.

How do I know which one is for me?

Have a look through the list below and see which one best suits you.

Are there any club rules?

Yes, each club has an *entrance requirement* of a short test you must take to be allowed to join! In addition, each club has its own bizarre rules, for example in the library of the Change

Agents club smoking is only allowed if you do not exhale and it is forbidden to return a book or learningbyte™ before the fine on it is due!

PentacleTheVBS.com/OrganisationalMagic.htm

In a world where we have grown weary of ineffective reorganisations that have the impact of increasing the staff turnover by an average of 83% – unfortunately the majority of whom are the ones we would rather keep hold of – this area is dedicated to training managers, human resource and personnel professionals and organisation development professionals.

In a world where most well known concepts such as segmentation, market share and markets are looking tired and jaded against the concept of individualised informatised offerings and reach.

AllChange.com

For project leaders, change agents, programme managers and other people who are trying to make difficult things happen involving a lot of other people.

This club's partner is Project Manager Today. The new world approach developed by Dr Eddie Obeng is used throughout.

PentacleTheVBS.com/NewWorldManager

This is the hot club for businesses trying to evolve into the New World. Aimed at entrepreneurs, intrapreneurs and high potentials. The focus here is making things happen in the New World in a New World way.

There are no club partners.

NewBusinessManagement

For trainers, management educators and developers, consultants and business school professors. This club is an area to learn how to teach new world topics, buy courses, share materials and collaborate on research.

PuttingStrategyToWork

In a world where any strategy that is designed to deliver benefits more than 18 months after the start has an 80% chance of failing to deliver most of its value, this club is designed for people who are accountable for the strange form of change that locks an organisation into a specific, prescribed and advantageous future. For directors, programme managers, programme directors, people who are in a sponsorship role, senior consultants.

Cybersenz

IT professionals, CIOs and knowledge managers.

MakingReengineeringHappen

For solution managers, supply chain managers.

More Copies

Sharing with Others

One of the key success criteria is to be able to educate and share the learning with the whole organisation.

To order more copies of *Never Reorganise Again!*

Number of copies	Price
1	£12.99
10	£120
50	£550
100	£1100
250	£2500

Join other NuvoMondists! Develop, find tools for and discuss your new organisation at PentacleTheVBS.com/OrganisationalMagic.htm

OTHER BOOKS BY EDDIE OBENG

New Rules for the New World
ISBN 1–900961–15–6

All Change!
ISBN 0 273 62221 8

Making Re-engineering Happen
ISBN 0 273 62220 X

Putting Strategy to Work
ISBN 0 273 60265 9

Soundbytes
ISBN 0 953 4869 0 7

Pentacle The Virtual Business School

Burke Lodge
20 London End
Beaconsfield
Bucks HP9 2JH
Tel +44 1494 678 555
Fax +44 1494 671 291
E-mail neveragain@pentaclethevbs.com
Web PentacleTheVBS.com/